THE KLONDIKE CAPITAL

Whitehorse

JILL FORAN

Published by Weigl Educational Publishers Limited
6325 – 10 Street SE
Calgary, Alberta, Canada
T2H 2Z9
Web site: http://www.weigl.com
Copyright © 2002 WEIGL EDUCATIONAL PUBLISHERS LIMITED

National Library of Canada Cataloguing in Publication Data
Foran, Jill.
 Whitehorse

 (Canadian Cities)
 Includes Index
 ISBN 1-894705-68-8

 1. Whitehorse (Yukon)--Juvenile literature. I. Title. II. Series:
Canadian Cities (Calgary, Alta)

Printed and bound in the United States of America
1 2 3 4 5 6 7 8 9 0   05 04 03 02 01

Senior Editor
Jared Keen
Copy Editor
Heather Kissock
Design
Warren Clark
Cover Design
Terry Paulhus
Layout
Katherine Phillips
Photo Researcher
Nicole Bezic King

We acknowledge the
financial support of
the Government of
Canada through the
Book Publishing
Industry Development
Program (BPIDP) for
our publishing activities.

Photograph Credits
Cathie Archbould, www.archbould.com: cover, inside cover, pages 4B, 5T, 5B, 7T, 8M, 9B, 13, 14, 16, 17, 19, 20T,
20B, 21, 29; Thies Bogner: page 10; Corel Corporation: page 24T,B; Lyn Hancock: pages 8B, 12, 15, 18, 22, 23,
25, 26, 27, 28; House of Commons: page 11; National Archives of Canada: pages 6B (PA53228), 7B (C39883), 8T
(PA202054); NFB/National Archives of Canada: page 9T; Yukon Archives, H. C. Barley Collection #5538: page 6T.

Every reasonable effort has been made to trace ownership and to obtain permission to reprint copyright material.
The publishers would be pleased to have any errors or omissions brought to their attention so that they may be
corrected in subsequent printings.

Contents

Introduction

Whitehorse is the capital of the Yukon Territory in the Canadian North. Situated in the southern part of the territory, Whitehorse serves as the financial, cultural, and commercial centre of the Yukon. The city is known for its magnificent setting, its friendly people, and for the many sporting events and festivals that it holds throughout the year.

Whitehorse

Canada

0   500 km

Getting There

Whitehorse is easily reached by land or air. Flights from Vancouver arrive at the Whitehorse International Airport on a daily basis. People who prefer to drive to the city can reach Whitehorse via the Alaska Highway.

At a Glance

Climate

Whitehorse has a dry climate, and it is known for its long, cold winters and short, cool summers. The city's average daily temperature in July ranges from 8° Celsius to 20°C. In January, the temperature ranges from –14°C to –23°C, but it can often drop to as low as –35°C. Besides being cold and long, winters in Whitehorse are also quite dark. At some points during the winter, Whitehorse has no more than 6 or 7 hours of daylight per day. However, during the summer months, the sun shines until very late at night. In fact, at the height of summer, the city enjoys about 20 hours of sunlight every day.

Area & Population

Whitehorse is situated on the west bank of the Yukon River, backed by a clay **escarpment**. The city of Whitehorse includes the downtown area, the community of McIntyre, several urban and rural subdivisions, and the industrial district of Maxwell. In all, Whitehorse covers an area of 414 square km, and about 23,500 people call the city home.

Wild Rapids and White Horses

Whitehorse earned its name from the wild, frothing rapids that lay just upstream from the early townsite. In the late nineteenth and early twentieth centuries, gold-seekers travelling to the Klondike region of the Yukon had to pass through these dangerous rapids before they could reach their destination. The swirling white water reminded early gold-seekers of the flowing manes of charging white horses. The foaming river became known as the Whitehorse Rapids, and the settlement was named Whitehorse. As the settlement grew and developed into a thriving transportation town, its unusual name became known throughout Canada and the United States.

Interesting Statistics

1. Whitehorse is the most westerly capital city in Canada.

2. About two-thirds of the Yukon's entire population lives in the Whitehorse area.

3. Whitehorse is Canada's third-largest city in terms of area.

4. Whitehorse is situated about 80 km north of the British Columbia border.

5. An experimental wind-turbine near Whitehorse produces enough energy each year to heat twenty-three homes.

The Past

Early Settlement

People have been frequenting the Whitehorse area for thousands of years. As early as 2,500 years ago, Native Peoples were setting up seasonal fishing and hunting camps in the region. These groups included the Southern Tutchone and Tagish

Trading posts were set up throughout the Whitehorse area during the gold rush.

peoples of the Yukon interior, and the Tlingit peoples from the Pacific coast. Although seasonal campsites were established year after year, permanent settlement in the Whitehorse area did not begin until the late nineteenth century.

On August 16, 1896, a discovery was made that would change Whitehorse forever. A large deposit of gold was found in Bonanza Creek, a **tributary** of the Yukon's Klondike River. Once word of the gold strike spread, thousands of **prospectors** from the United States and elsewhere journeyed to the Klondike region looking to get rich. Parts of the journey were very challenging due to the Yukon's often-treacherous terrain. Among the most dangerous obstacles were Miles Canyon and the Whitehorse Rapids, two rushing channels along the Yukon River. Many prospectors risked their lives as they tried to cross these violent rapids. Just beyond the rapids lay the Whitehorse townsite, which soon became a temporary stopping point for exhausted prospectors who had survived the crossing.

Key Events

500 BCE Native Peoples use the Whitehorse area as a seasonal campsite.

1895 A detachment of the North West Mounted Police is sent to police the Yukon.

1896 Skookum Jim, Tagish Charlie, and George Washington Carmack discover gold in a tributary of the Klondike River.

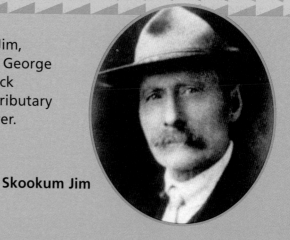

Skookum Jim

Government

Whitehorse had no form of local government until the middle of the twentieth century. For more than fifty years, it was managed primarily by the territorial government, which was located in Dawson City. Because of its location near the Klondike, the once tiny outpost of Dawson had turned into one of western Canada's largest cities by May of 1898. That summer, the federal government made the Yukon district a separate territory of Canada, naming Dawson City as capital. By 1908, an elected ten-member council based in Dawson City administered all of the Yukon, including Whitehorse.

The Yukon experienced an enormous population decline when the gold rush came to an end in the early 1900s. In 1919, due to the shrinking population, the federal government reduced the number of territorial council members to three. As the years passed, the population of Dawson City continued to drop, while in Whitehorse, things were looking up. Increased development, including the construction of the Alaska Highway in the 1940s, brought more businesses and settlers to the town. In 1950, Whitehorse was declared a city. That year, the people of Whitehorse elected their first municipal government. In 1953, Whitehorse was made the new capital of the Yukon, and the territorial government moved to the city, where it continues to meet today.

Whitehorse City Hall is home to the mayor's office and the rest of the municipal government.

1897 The Klondike Gold Rush begins.

1898 The Yukon is made a separate territory of Canada, and Dawson City is named the capital.

1900 Construction is completed on the White Pass and Yukon Route Railway, providing for easier shipment of goods and people to the North.

Law and Order

The Royal Canadian Mounted Police (RCMP) have been maintaining order in Whitehorse and the rest of the Yukon for more than 100 years. Until the late nineteenth century, the Yukon's population consisted mostly of Native Peoples and a small number of European fur traders. In the 1870s, the population increased as miners began to arrive in search of gold. During this time, the Yukon had no system of civil authority, and fights frequently broke out between American and Canadian prospectors over the right to gold claims. In 1895, in order to avoid further disorder and assert Canadian authority in the area, the federal government sent a **detachment** of nineteen North West Mounted Police (NWMP)—now known as the RCMP—to the Yukon district. When the gold rush began in 1897, the

The North West Mounted Police demonstrate their riding abilities.

number of police was doubled, and strict rules were set out in order to control the flood of incoming prospectors. The NWMP worked out of a variety of posts throughout the territory. For many years, their post at Whitehorse was located in the railway depot.

In 1943, the headquarters of the Yukon division of the RCMP were moved from Dawson City to Whitehorse. Today, the RCMP "M" Division is still based in Whitehorse, and it continues to function as the main policing unit for the entire Yukon territory.

Key Events

1920 The first aircraft in the Yukon lands at Whitehorse.

1927 Whitehorse gets its first commercial airline—The Yukon Airways and Exploration Company.

1942 Construction of the Alaska Highway begins, bringing thousands of people to the Whitehorse area. The highway is completed within 8 months.

Early Transportation

The development of transportation routes began in the Yukon as a result of the Klondike Gold Rush. The territory's remote location made getting to the Klondike River very difficult.

In 1898, a group of businessmen decided to build a railway. It was agreed that the railway would begin in Skagway, Alaska, and that its **terminus** would be at Whitehorse. On July 29, 1900, the White Pass and Yukon Route Railway was completed. It immediately improved the movement of goods and people to and from the Yukon. Whitehorse soon developed from a temporary camping site into a sizeable town and a busy transportation hub.

The Alaska Highway

Although the Yukon was far from the action of World War II, the war still had a major effect on Whitehorse. After the Japanese attack on Pearl Harbor in 1941, the U.S. became fearful of more attacks along the Pacific coast. In order to strengthen its defences, the U.S. government received permission to build a highway through Canadian territory that would connect Alaska with the lower states. This highway would allow goods and soldiers to be carried by land to various outposts and airfields, thereby lessening the threat of attack along the coast. Construction of the 2,500-km highway began in March of 1942. More than 11,000 American soldiers and 16,000 American and Canadian civilian workers poured into Whitehorse to work on the road. The building crews worked northward and southward until the highway, stretching from British Columbia to Alaska, was completed. Called the Alaska Highway, this long stretch of road was instrumental in Whitehorse's growth and development.

Construction of the Alaska Highway created jobs and provided a much-needed transport link.

1943 The headquarters of the Yukon subdivision of the RCMP are transferred from Dawson City to Whitehorse.

1950 Whitehorse becomes a city, and the first mayor and council are elected.

1953 Whitehorse is made the capital of the Yukon.

Famous People

Pierre Berton
1920—

Pierre Berton is one of Canada's most celebrated non-fiction writers. Born in Whitehorse, Pierre spent most of his childhood years in Dawson City. His father was a gold-seeker during the Klondike Gold Rush, and his mother, Laura, was both a schoolteacher and respected writer.

Pierre left the Yukon in the 1930s, and during World War II, he spent almost four years in the Canadian army. After serving his country, he moved to Vancouver to begin a career in journalism. At the age of 21, Pierre became the youngest city editor ever to work on a Canadian daily newspaper. In 1947, he moved to Toronto and soon became the managing editor of *Maclean's* magazine. Pierre's first book was published in 1958. Called *Klondike*, it explores in detail the events of the Klondike Gold Rush. The book, which was widely popular and highly acclaimed, received a governor general's award, one of Canada's top literary prizes. Since then, Pierre has gone on to write more than thirty-nine books, many of which deal with aspects of Canadian history.

Ted Harrison 1926—

Ted Harrison is one of Canada's most popular visual artists. Born in the village of Wingate, England, Ted travelled around the world teaching art before moving to the Yukon in 1967. He and his family lived in Carcross until 1970 then moved to Whitehorse, where he taught art until 1979. That year, he decided to devote most of his time to working on his own art. Ted's life in the Yukon has been the inspiration for much of his artwork. Many of his most celebrated paintings depict the beautiful scenery and fascinating people of the territory. His work can be seen in galleries and museums throughout Canada, as well as in countries around the world. Ted has also written and illustrated several popular children's books. In 1987, he received the Order of Canada for his contribution to the development of Canadian culture.

Florence Whyard 1917–

Florence Whyard is a well-known author, publisher, and politician in Whitehorse. Born in London, Ontario, Florence trained World War II pilots before moving to Yellowknife in 1945. While there, Florence had three children, became very active in community organizations, worked as a freelance writer, and served as program manager for a community radio station. In 1954, Florence and her family moved to Whitehorse, where she continued her career in journalism as a freelance writer and the editor of the *Whitehorse Star*. In 1981, she was elected mayor of Whitehorse and served a successful term. Then, from 1988 to 1995,

Florence served as Administrator of the Yukon. During that time, she also formed her own publishing house and went on to produce a variety of fascinating books about the Yukon. Over the years, Florence has received many awards and honours.

Audrey McLaughlin 1936–

Audrey McLaughlin was the first woman to lead a major federal political party in Canada. Originally from Dutton, Ontario, Audrey moved to Whitehorse in 1979. Once there, she opened her own consulting business. Audrey worked to improve child welfare legislation in the Yukon, and she became involved with Native land-

claims research. Audrey also became active in local election campaigns for the New Democratic Party (NDP). In 1987, Audrey was elected to the federal House of Commons for the Yukon. Two years later, she was elected the first female leader of the NDP party, a position she held until 1995.

Elijah Smith 1912–1991

Elijah Smith was a prominent Native-rights activist. Born in Hutshi Village, Yukon, Elijah worked as a trapper and fisher. He also served in the Canadian Armed Forces during World War II. After the war, Elijah devoted his life to the unification and advancement of the Yukon's Native Peoples. During his career, Elijah held many important positions, including Chief of the Kwanlin Dun band in Whitehorse, founding president of the Yukon Native Brotherhood, founding chairman of the Council for Yukon Indians, and the Yukon representative of the National Indian Brotherhood. Elijah received many awards for his dedication to Native rights.

Culture

The Arts

Whitehorse has a lively arts scene. Through the years, artists of all types have been inspired by the area's breathtaking beauty, its exciting history, and its rich cultural heritage. Music, dance, theatre, and visual arts all thrive in the city.

Whitehorse is home to several world-class visual artists. Many of their works can be found in galleries and museums in the city. One of the most popular galleries is located in the Yukon Arts Centre. This complex also houses a 430-seat auditorium that serves as the city's theatre and concert hall, where plays, dance performances, and musical events are held. Other plays and performances can be enjoyed at Guild Hall and in the Nakai Theatre.

One of the most popular theatrical events in Whitehorse is the Frantic Follies. Performed every summer evening at the Westmark Whitehorse Hotel, this entertaining show features professional actors, dancers, and musicians who recapture the gold-rush era. With comical skits, songs, and high-kicking cancan dances, these performers bring the stage shows of the late 1890s back to life.

The Frantic Follies made its professional debut on June 16, 1970.

FESTIVALS

Whitehorse holds a variety of festivals and events throughout the year. In early February, the city hosts the only winter music festival in the country. Called the **Frostbite Music Festival**, this event features local musicians as well as performers from all over Canada and parts of the U.S. For two days and three nights, audiences can hear all kinds of music, including jazz, rock and roll, country, folk, blues, and traditional Native songs. The festival also features music workshops and entertainment for children. Later in February, the city holds the **Yukon Sourdough Rendez-Vous**. This week-long event celebrates the approaching end of winter and features a wide range of unique

Holiday Fun

People in Whitehorse like to celebrate, and they mark the year's most important occasions with all sorts of exciting festivities. On June 21, the city celebrates National Aboriginal Day with several events that honour Native culture. The day's celebrations begin with a lively parade and continue with cultural activities, including Native dancing, drumming, and singing.

Saint-Jean Baptiste Day is also celebrated in Whitehorse. St. Jean Baptiste is the patron saint of French Canadians, and on June 24, **Francophones** across Canada honour him with various festivals and celebrations. In Whitehorse, people of French descent have celebrated Saint-Jean Baptiste Day since 1905, and events for the holiday include live music, dancing, food, and many family activities.

On July 1, Whitehorse holds an enormous celebration to mark Canada's birthday. Activities include a parade, a pancake breakfast, live entertainment, cultural events, citizenship ceremonies, and the Yukon River Rubber Duck Race. As the weather gets colder and December approaches, the people of Whitehorse prepare to celebrate the Christmas season. The city is lit up with thousands of Christmas lights, and local choirs, schools, church groups, and theatre troupes present festive Christmas concerts and pageants.

Native dramas re-enact the stories and history of the Whitehorse area.

entertainment. Downtown streets are blocked off for games and hilarious events such as a flour-packing contest, a tug-a-truck contest, an axe-throwing contest, and a chainsaw-chucking contest. The festival also features dancing, live music, a fiddlers' show, an air show, and a costume contest.

One of the largest annual events in Whitehorse is the **Yukon International Storytelling Festival**. Held every year at the end of May, this festival features storytellers, dancers, and drummers from around the world who come together to celebrate the rich storytelling tradition of the North. Audiences at the festival are treated to fascinating Native myths and legends told by these expert storytellers.

Food

Buying food in Whitehorse can often be more expensive than buying food in other Canadian cities. With only a small amount of fertile land and an extremely short growing season, the Yukon is severely limited in its agricultural output. This means that produce and processed foods must often be shipped north from other provinces. As a result of the long distances and the costs involved, items in the supermarkets can be quite expensive. While farming is not a major activity in the Yukon, many small farms manage to grow produce for local markets. Vegetables are grown in greenhouses during the long summer days, and some field crops grow well in certain areas of the territory. Farmers in the Whitehorse area also raise and sell livestock to

Dining out in Whitehorse gives visitors a chance to try new foods.

local markets. Fishing and hunting provide local food sources as well. Many people in Whitehorse enjoy freshly caught salmon, whitefish, and game, such as moose and deer.

At the end of every August, the people of Whitehorse gather at Rotary Park for the Klondyke Harvest Fair. This festival celebrates the perseverance of local gardeners and farmers who have managed to grow produce in the challenging environment of the Canadian North. A farmers' market at the fair sells everything from locally grown fruits and vegetables to baked goods, preserves, and craftwork. Many of Whitehorse's restaurants also feature local produce in their dishes. The city is home to several restaurants, which serve everything from fast food to traditional Northern fare.

Mooseburgers

1 kg ground moose meat
1 egg
500 mL (2 cups) bread crumbs
salt and pepper
pinch of garlic
125 mL (1/2 cup) steak sauce
or barbeque sauce

Mix ingredients together in a large bowl. Form into patties, and cook in a frying pan or on the barbeque until they are well done. Place each patty in a hamburger bun, and add your favourite fixings. Enjoy!

Cultural Groups

People in Whitehorse come from many different ethnic backgrounds. Throughout the first half of the twentieth century, people from all over Canada and parts of the U.S. travelled to Whitehorse to work in nearby mines or to take part in one of the area's major construction projects.

Today, the majority of Whitehorse's population is made up of people who came from other parts of Canada. In fact, only about 30 percent of the city's residents were actually born in the Yukon.

Whitehorse is also home to a significant number of Native Peoples. About 15 percent of the city's population is of Native descent. Two prominent Native groups have their homes in the Whitehorse area. The Kwanlin Dun are based in McIntyre, which is a subdivision of Whitehorse. This group is an **amalgamation** of many Yukon Native groups, including people from the Northern and Southern Tutchone groups, as well as the Tagish. The Kwanlin Dun population numbers about 1,000, and its members work hard to preserve and share their many cultural traditions. A group of about 200 people known as the Ta'an Kwach'an also has members who are Southern Tutchone and Tagish. This group lives primarily in the Lake Laberge area.

Native craftspeople sell their artwork in shops and at art stalls throughout the city.

Long Ago Peoples Place

Thousands of years ago, long before European explorers began to arrive in the Yukon, the territory was home to several Native groups. These groups moved from place to place, following animal patterns and setting up temporary campsites along traditional routes. Today, the lifestyles of these early Native groups are depicted at Kwaday Dan Kenji, a re-creation of a traditional First Nations camp. In English, Kwaday Dan Kenji translates as "Long Ago Peoples Place." This place was designed to help share a part of the territory's rich Native history, and it provides visitors with a better understanding of how the Yukon's early peoples lived.

The Economy

Mining has always played an important role in the economy of Whitehorse.

Gaining Stability

Mining has always played an important role in the economy of Whitehorse. Throughout its history, the city has served as the main transportation and service base for the Yukon's mining industry. Although mining is still vital to both the city and the territory, the Yukon's mineral production varies greatly from year to year. Mines in the territory have been opened, closed, and even re-opened, all in response to demand for metal ores in the world marketplace. As a result of the instability of the mining industry, Whitehorse's economy has weathered several ups and downs.

When Whitehorse was declared the capital of the Yukon in 1953, government services replaced mining as the city's major economic sector. Moving the territorial government from Dawson City helped attract more people and businesses to Whitehorse. The move also created new jobs for people in the area, providing more stability to the city's unpredictable economy. Today, three levels of government—municipal, territorial, and federal—employ more than 21 percent of the city's work force. Government employees in Whitehorse work in a wide range of jobs. Some are politicians or public figures, while others hold positions as clerks, secretaries, scientists, mapmakers, or caretakers.

At the legislature building in Whitehorse, officials meet to discuss economic and political issues.

Serving the Territory

Government workers in Whitehorse are part of the city's wide-ranging service sector. This sector employs more people than any other industrial sector in the city. As the largest community in the Yukon, Whitehorse has a number of services that other communities in the territory do not have. Many people from more remote areas must travel to Whitehorse to buy supplies, visit a dentist, or even watch a movie. Because it is the territory's main service and supply centre, the city is home to a wide range of businesses and facilities that cater to most needs.

Tourism is another vital part of the city's service industry. An estimated $124 million is earned from tourism each year, and 2,000 people are employed in tourism-related jobs in the territory. Thousands of visitors travel to the Yukon to take in its beautiful scenery and enjoy its vast wilderness. As the territory's

Many of Whitehorse's shops feature replica items from the days of the gold rush.

More people are employed in the service sector than in any other industry in Whitehorse.

transportation hub, Whitehorse serves as a gateway to the rest of the Yukon, and most visitors spend time touring the city and its various attractions. Whitehorse offers these visitors a full range of services, including hotels, restaurants, souvenir stores, and outfitting companies.

A trolley takes visitors and residents on a waterfront tour of Whitehorse.

Getting Around in Whitehorse

One of the best ways to get around in Whitehorse is to walk. Although it has several surrounding communities, the downtown core is small, and many of the city's popular attractions and businesses are located within easy walking distance of each other. Streets in the city run in an east-west direction, while avenues run north to south. One of the busiest and most colourful streets in Whitehorse is Main Street, which runs directly through the centre of the downtown area. Other busy traffic routes include Second and Fourth avenues.

The threat of air pollution has played a significant role in how some people in Whitehorse choose to get around. Many people in the city are concerned about polluting the air and, as a result, have chosen not to drive their cars. As an alternative to driving, many citizens make use of the city's public transportation system. Called Whitehorse Transit, this system began operating in 1976 and has been providing bus transportation throughout the city ever since. For those who prefer to walk or cycle, Whitehorse also has an extensive system of trails that link most parts of the city.

Touring by Road, Rail, or River

Many companies in Whitehorse offer scenic tours of the city and its surrounding areas. Gray Line Yukon, a bus line that provides transportation from Whitehorse to other northern communities, also offers a city tour that takes passengers to historical points of interest in the area. More historical sites can be seen while boating on the Yukon River. Riverboat tours bring passengers past many of the remains from the gold-rush era. These remains include the remnants of a wooden tramway built to carry gold-rush supplies across the rapids, as well as the site of Canyon City, a temporary town set up by prospectors while they constructed boats to travel along the river. Visitors who wish to gain a further glimpse into the past can take a tour on the White Pass and Yukon Route Railway. In a refurbished, comfortable train, passengers can ride along the route that was once travelled by thousands of hopeful prospectors.

A Centre for Learning

Whitehorse is the main centre for education in the Yukon. The city has ten elementary schools, one of which offers a French immersion program. There are also three secondary schools in Whitehorse, as well as a French-language school that offers both elementary and secondary education. Like other schools throughout the Yukon, those in Whitehorse follow the **curriculum** set out by the British Columbia Ministry of Education. This means that students in Whitehorse and other Yukon communities may write British Columbia departmental exams.

Whitehorse is also home to the main campus of Yukon College—the territory's only post-secondary institution. Formed in 1983, Yukon College offers programs in several subject areas, including trades and

Whitehorse is home to the main campus of Yukon College.

technology, business administration, and computer sciences. The college also offers several university courses and programs, and students there can earn university degrees in a variety of fields. In all, about 6,000 students throughout the territory are enrolled in programs at Yukon College. In 1988, the college moved its Whitehorse campus to a new location at Yukon Place, in the suburb of Takhini. This new campus, called Ayamdigut, houses many excellent facilities, including modern classrooms, laboratories, computer stations, and student residences.

At Yukon College, students take classes to prepare for their chosen careers.

Sports and Recreation

Cycling is a great way to explore the area around Whitehorse.

Outdoor Fun

Residents and visitors in Whitehorse enjoy a near-endless variety of recreational activities. In the summer, hikers and cyclists make use of the city's local trails and pathways, as well as the many challenging mountain trails found nearby. Grey Mountain is one of the most popular spots for hikers and mountain bikers. Rock climbers and ice climbers enjoy the excellent climbing opportunities at places such as the Rock Gardens and the Golden Canyon. For those who prefer water sports, the Yukon River is ideal for canoeing, kayaking, and white-water rafting.

Other popular summertime activities in Whitehorse include horseback riding, fishing, and golfing.

In the winter, the city's outdoor enthusiasts keep busy with a whole new list of activities. Snowmobiling is popular among many people in Whitehorse, and the city offers about 300 km of snowmobile trails. There are also a number of well-kept cross-country ski trails around Whitehorse, as well as plenty of opportunities for challenging backcountry skiing. The Mount Sima Skiing Area offers excellent downhill skiing and snowboarding, with eight groomed runs. Other popular winter sports include dog mushing, ice fishing, and skating.

Ice surfing on Lake Scwatka is a popular winter pastime.

Competitive Events

Many people in Whitehorse participate in competitive sports. The city has amateur leagues that allow citizens of all ages to take part in sports such as hockey, soccer, baseball, swimming, skiing, and curling. There are also a few professional sports teams based in Whitehorse, including two popular hockey teams—the Whitehorse Huskies of the Supreme Inter-Continental Hockey League, and the Yukon Claim Jumpers of the Nor-Pac Hockey League.

Whitehorse also hosts a number of exciting athletic competitions throughout the year, drawing talented athletes from around the city and from other parts of the country as well. In June, the Yukon River Quest features teams of two paddlers in canoes and kayaks racing 700 km down the Yukon River from Whitehorse to Dawson City. The Whitehorse Rodeo takes place every July at the Rodeo Grounds along the North Klondike Highway. There, cowboys compete in a series of events, including bull riding, calf roping, and pack-horse racing. Later in the summer, the Klondike Trail of '98 International Road Relay is held between Skagway, Alaska, and Whitehorse. Runners at this event race day and night along a 176-km route once used by prospectors during the Klondike Gold Rush. All of Whitehorse's athletic events draw large crowds of spectators, who gather to cheer on the athletes and to take part in the fun.

The Yukon Quest

The Yukon Quest is one of the toughest and best-known dogsled races in the world. Every February, North America's top mushers compete in this race, which stretches for 1,600 km between Whitehorse and Fairbanks, Alaska. The Yukon Quest retraces the harsh wilderness route first used by prospectors during the gold rush, and it is a true test of **endurance**. Each team in the quest consists of one musher, one sled, and between eight and fourteen dogs. The sleds must carry all the equipment that the mushers and the dogs will need, including food, a heavy sleeping bag, a hand-axe, snowshoes, veterinary records, and at least eight sets of dog booties. The race's starting point alternates yearly between Whitehorse and Fairbanks, and teams can take anywhere from ten to twenty days to complete the course. The Yukon Quest is such a challenge that, although most mushers and their dogs spend all year preparing for the event, only about two-thirds of the competitors actually finish the race.

Tourism

Sharing History

Downtown Whitehorse has two museums that introduce visitors to the rich history of the Yukon. The MacBride Museum offers an in-depth look at the territory's natural and cultural heritage with a variety of fascinating exhibits. Located on the banks of the Yukon River, the museum takes up half a city block and features a main exhibition building, as well as a vehicle display garage, a blacksmith's shed, and two important historical structures—a government telegraph office from 1900 and the cabin of a well-known prospector named Sam McGee. The main building at the museum houses four permanent galleries that explore many aspects of the territory's history, including its early Native Peoples, the Klondike Gold Rush, the presence of the RCMP, and the natural and industrial history of the area. One of the most popular exhibits is the Rivers of Gold, which features the largest public collection of Yukon gold in Canada.

The MacBride Museum also offers several interactive programs for visitors. These include heritage lectures, artisan workshops, and the opportunity to pan for gold using the same techniques that the prospectors used during the gold rush.

Just a short walk away from the MacBride Museum is the Old Log Church Museum. Housed in one of the oldest buildings in Whitehorse, this museum features fascinating exhibits on the Yukon's early explorers, missionaries, church history, and Native culture.

The MacBride Museum showcases the natural and cultural history of the Yukon.

Planes, Trains, and Ancient History

Tourists interested in exploring the development of travel in the territory can visit the Yukon Transportation Museum. Located on the Alaska Highway next to the airport, this museum houses many historic artifacts that were once used to get around in the North. Items on display include moose-skin boats, snowshoes, dogsleds, stagecoaches, and a full-size replica of the territory's first commercial aircraft—the *Queen of the Yukon*. The museum also has exhibits that depict the territory's gold-rush transportation heritage, as well as displays on the construction of the Alaska Highway. A mural on the exterior wall of the museum, painted by local artists, beautifully depicts the many modes of transportation that have been used through the years.

Other aspects of the Yukon's rich history can be discovered at the Beringia Interpretive Centre, next door to the Yukon Transportation Museum. This centre introduces visitors to the world of the Yukon during the last Ice Age. The territory's ancient past is explored through fascinating murals and **dioramas** representing the ancient landscapes and strange animals that once dominated the North. Visitors to the centre can inspect life-size replicas of extinct animals such as the woolly mammoth, the scimitar cat, and the giant beaver.

During the gold rush, prospectors relied on a number of transportation modes, including boat, sled, and foot.

SS Klondike II

One of the most popular attractions in Whitehorse is the SS *Klondike II*. **Berthed** at the end of 2nd Avenue, the SS *Klondike II* was the largest and the last of the **sternwheelers** to carry goods on the Yukon River. Now a national historic site, this impressive boat was a copy of the original SS *Klondike*, which was built in 1929 but sank in 1936 when it struck a reef. The SS *Klondike II* was launched in 1937. Today, the sternwheeler has been restored to its 1937 appearance, and tourists can climb aboard and explore more than 7,000 artifacts that are on display.

Kluane National Park

Kluane National Park and Reserve is located 170 km west of Whitehorse, on the Alaska Highway. The park encompasses more than 22,000 sq km of breathtaking wilderness. It is dominated by the St. Elias Mountains, which feature some of the highest peaks in North America, including Mount Logan—the tallest mountain in Canada. Kluane National Park is also home to some of the largest non-polar ice fields in the world, as well as an extensive network of glaciers, countless mountain lakes, beautiful alpine meadows, and swift-running rivers. Each year, thousands of tourists drive from Whitehorse to Kluane National Park to enjoy day or overnight adventures. Hiking, white-water rafting, helicopter tours, and mountain climbing are among the many outdoor activities that visitors take pleasure in while at Kluane. Many others travel to the park

Caribou, also known as reindeer, can be found in and around the Whitehorse area.

just to see the incredible range of wildlife species that thrive there. Golden eagles, ptarmigans, Dall sheep, caribou, moose, and one of the world's largest populations of grizzly bears are all found at Kluane.

Tourists who would like to view wildlife without having to drive too far out of Whitehorse can visit the Yukon Game Farm and Wildlife Preserve. Situated about 25 km north of the city, this large park is dedicated to the breeding and conservation of northern mammals such as elk, mule deer, moose, caribou, wood bison, musk-ox, and mountain goats. Visitors can see these animals in their natural habitats as they tour the preserve's 300 hectares of forests, meadows, and marshes.

Although a threatened species, the grizzly bear is the Yukon's most powerful animal.

The Whitehorse Fishway is full of Chinook salmon from late July until early September.

Springs and Ladders

The Takhini Hot Springs are one of the most relaxing attractions that the Whitehorse area has to offer. Located about 30 km north of the city, these natural mineral-water springs feed into a large, outdoor pool surrounded by beautiful Yukon scenery. The hot springs maintain the temperature of the pool at about 36°C, making it a perfect spot for year-round swimming and relaxing. Even in the middle of winter, visitors can swim in the pool and take in the beauty of their snowy surroundings without getting the least bit cold.

For an altogether different kind of water activity, tourists can visit the Whitehorse Fishway in the suburban area of Riverdale. Built in 1959, the fishway was designed to allow migrating salmon in the Yukon River to bypass the newly constructed Whitehorse Dam, which otherwise would have blocked their path. Every summer, hundreds of Chinook salmon swim through the fishway to reach their spawning grounds in southern Yukon. The Whitehorse Fishway features a fish-ladder that stretches for 366 m, making it the longest wooden fish-ladder in the world. Water surging from the fishway attracts the fish into the ladder, where they then must leap over the partitions that separate each ladder "step," or swim through the underground doorways in each partition.

The Yukon Gardens

Growing gardens in a northern climate is often quite a challenge. However, because of the long summer days enjoyed in the North, many beautiful plants and flowers do manage to thrive there. A number of these plants can be seen at the Yukon Gardens— the only botanical gardens in the Canadian North. Located in Whitehorse, the Yukon Gardens feature large displays of wild plants, hardy vegetables, fruit trees, and several species of flowers, including seventeen varieties of wild orchids. Plant-lovers will enjoy exploring the gardens, which also feature an excellent garden shopping centre where visitors may purchase plants, flowers, and produce native to the territory.

Architecture

Early Architecture and the Old Log Church

As one of Canada's youngest cities, Whitehorse has very few buildings that predate the early 1900s. Most of the city's early structures, as well as many of its more modern buildings, are constructed of either logs or milled lumber. The city's oldest buildings, be they businesses or homes, are all known for their modest, unimposing designs and cottage-like appearances.

The oldest building still in use in Whitehorse is the Old Log Church. Before the church was built in 1900, Whitehorse's first priest held church services in a tent, and he and his wife lived in another tent nearby. With the construction of the new log building, Whitehorse received its very first church, and by 1901,

a two-storey log **rectory** was built for the priest and his wife. As the years passed, several additions were made to both the church and the rectory. In 1916, a **vestry** adjoining the church was enlarged, and by 1945, the church had a new porch, cloakroom, and **belfry**. In 1953, the log church was officially named the Cathedral Church of the Diocese, giving it the distinction of being the very first log cathedral in the world. Although church services are no longer offered at the Old Log Church, the structure houses an important museum and continues to serve as a well-built reminder of the city's earliest architectural styles.

Many of the oldest buildings in Whitehorse are made of logs.

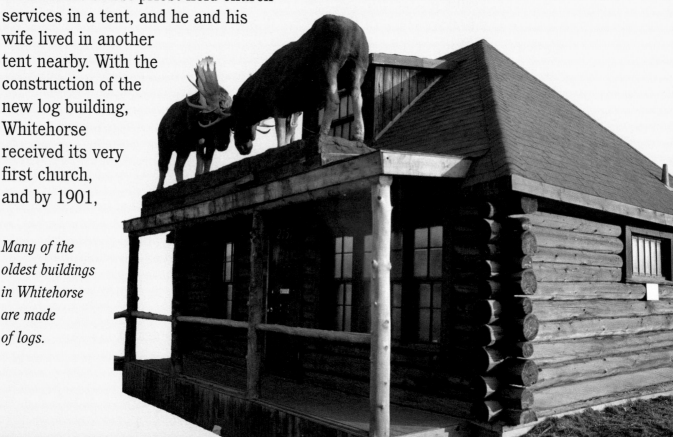

Log Cabin Skyscrapers

During the construction of the Alaska Highway, Whitehorse was overflowing with army and construction personnel. This **influx** of people led to a shortage of rental space in the city. Every hotel and home in the area was full, and even riverboats took in overnight guests to help with the overcrowding problem. The shortage of accommodation during the 1940s prompted many people to build small cabins that they could rent to others. One of these builders was a man named Martin Berrigan. While in his seventies, Berrigan built and rented out a number of log cabins, including what are now the two best-known structures in the city—the log skyscrapers. Built in 1947, the "skyscrapers" consist of two log structures: one two-storey cabin and one three-storey cabin. The three-storey structure is the more impressive of the two, consisting of four small cabins piled on top of one another. It stands fifty-eight logs high, with each log weighing more than 135 kg. Today, both skyscrapers have been renovated into individual apartments, and they remain the most-photographed buildings in Whitehorse.

Whitehorse's log skyscrapers were built by Martin Berrigan, an area resident.

WP & YR Railway Station

One of the most prominent historical buildings in Whitehorse is the White Pass and Yukon Route (WP & YR) railway depot. Originally built in 1900, the depot looked very much like depots in other Canadian towns during the early part of the twentieth century. It was a large, two-storeyed wooden structure, and its size and handsome exterior made it stand out against other buildings in the town. For many years, the depot accommodated railway offices, a customs house, and the North West Mounted Police station. In 1905, it was destroyed in a fire that also ruined most of Whitehorse's other commercial buildings. However, within two months, a new station resembling its **predecessor** was constructed on the very same site. For almost eighty years, this depot served as the formal entry point for all goods and passengers arriving by rail from Alaska. In the 1950s, the depot underwent a substantial facelift when it received an extension to its second storey and log siding along its exterior.

As time passed, the Yukon became more and more accessible by road and air, and the railway became less of a necessity. In 1982, the WP & YR Railway stopped running, and the depot's role as a gateway came to an end. Today, the railway station is part of the Canadian Register of Heritage Properties.

Fascinating Facts

1 Every August, people in motorized bathtubs race along the Yukon River during Whitehorse's annual NMI Mobility Yukon River Bathtub Race. This race, which stretches for more than 780 km, is one of the longest and most challenging bathtub races in the world.

2 The Kwanlin Dun is the largest Native group in Whitehorse. The group's name translates as "people of the rapids."

3 Whitehorse enjoyed a "copper rush" during the same time as the famous Klondike Gold Rush. In 1898, a prospector on his way to Dawson City discovered a rich supply of copper near Whitehorse and immediately staked a claim. By the next year, copper mining activity in the area was attracting several prospectors who had originally come to the territory in search of gold.

4 The Yukon River is the fourth-longest river in North America.

5 The Whitehorse International Airport is home to the world's largest weather vane. This instrument is made from an airplane mounted on a rotating pedestal. It helps the people of Whitehorse determine which way the wind is blowing.

6 In the early 1900s, Whitehorse's name was almost changed to Closeleigh. This new name was meant to honour the Close Brothers, who provided money for the construction of the White Pass and Yukon Route railway. The Yukon's commissioner, William Ogilvie, overruled the proposed name change due to the fact that the original name was already so well established.

7 In Whitehorse, as in the rest of the territory, a "sourdough" is someone who has survived a Yukon winter. Until newcomers to the territory have lived through their first Yukon winter, they are traditionally referred to as "Cheechakos" or "greenhorns."

8 Whitehorse is one of the best locations in Canada for viewing the northern lights, or aurora borealis.

9 Whitehorse has two sister cities—Echuca, Australia, and Juneau, Alaska.

10 The first commercial airline in the Yukon was based in Whitehorse during the 1920s. Called the Yukon Airways and Exploration Company, its first airplane was said to be the only commercial aircraft with charcoal foot warmers at the time. The airplane was named the *Queen of the Yukon*, and it was the sister aircraft to Charles Lindberg's *Spirit of St. Louis*.

Activities

30

Based on what you have read, try to answer the following questions.

Multiple Choice

1 In what year was Whitehorse declared the capital of the Yukon?
a. 1898
b. 1900
c. 1950
d. 1953

2 Who built Whitehorse's log skyscrapers?
a. Elijah Smith
b. Martin Berrigan
c. Florence Whyard
d. Ted Harrison

3 At which Whitehorse festival can spectators watch a chainsaw-chucking competition?
a. The Sourdough Rendez-Vous Festival
b. The Frostbite Music Festival
c. The Yukon International Storytelling Festival
d. The Klondyke Harvest Festival

4 The largest collection of Yukon gold in Canada is on display at:
a. The Old Log Church Museum
b. The MacBride Museum
c. The Beringia Interpretive Centre
d. The Yukon Transportation Museum

5 What was the name of the Yukon's first commercial aircraft?
a. SS *Klondike*
b. *White Pass and Yukon*
c. *Queen of the Yukon*
d. *Spirit of St. Louis*

True or False

6 Whitehorse is home to the only botanical gardens in northern Canada.

7 Most of the people living in Whitehorse were born in the Yukon.

8 Mount Logan, situated in Kluane National Park, is Canada's highest peak.

9 The Alaska Highway was built to make travelling easier for gold-seekers.

10 Whitehorse has the largest wooden fish-ladder in the world.

Answers: 1. d. 1953 2. b. Martin Berrigan 3. a. The Sourdough Rendez-Vous Festival 4. b. The MacBride Museum 5. *Queen of the Yukon* 6. True 7. False. Only 30 percent were born in the Yukon. 8. True 9. False. The highway was built to help enforce U.S. defences against Japanese attack during World War II. 10. True

More Information

Books

Lourie, Peter. **Yukon River**. Honesdale, Pennsylvania: Boyds Mill Press, 1992.

Parker, Janice. **Eye on Canada: Yukon**. Calgary: Weigl Educational Publishers, 2001.

Pynn, Larry. **The Forgotten Trail**. Toronto: Doubleday, 1996.

Web sites

City of Whitehorse

http://www.city.whitehorse.yk.ca

MacBride Museum

http://www.macbridemuseum.com

Yukon Beringia Interpretive Centre

http://www.beringia.com

Kwaday Dan Kenji homepage

http://www.cafn.yk.net/kwaday.htm

History of Whitehorse

http://www.yukonalaska.com/communities/whitehorsehist.html

Some Web sites stay current longer than others. To find information on Yellowknife, use your Internet search engine to look up topics such as "Nakai Theatre," "Klondyke Harvest Festival," "Mount Logan," or any other topic you want to research.

Glossary

amalgamation: a unification or merger

belfry: a bell tower

berthed: docked

curriculum: the courses and topics studied in school

detachment: a body of troops

dioramas: life-size displays representing scenes from nature or history

endurance: the ability to continue despite exhaustion or difficulty

escarpment: a steep slope or cliff

Francophones: people who speak French

influx: the arrival of people or objects in large numbers

predecessor: something that came before

prospectors: gold-seekers

rectory: a house for clergy

sternwheelers: boats that are propelled by a paddlewheel at the rear

terminus: the end of a railway line

tributary: a river or stream that joins a larger body of water

vestry: a room or building attached to a church where robes are kept

Index